Tying Bass Flies
12 of the Best

Deke Meyer

Frank
Amato
PORTLAND

Welcome To *Tying Bass Flies*

Through step-by-step photos and description this book will show you how to tie the dozen best bass flies, effective variations of the basic recipes, and tips on how to fish these flies.

There are countless coves in large reservoirs, appealing little lakes, and pastoral farm ponds all across the country just waiting for an angler to entice their resident bass with a well placed fly. As prime gamefish and superior predators, largemouth, smallmouth and spotted bass readily attack flies, whether topwater poppers or subsurface streamers.

The key to catching bass on a fly is to impart the impression of bulky prey, but without trying to cast a jumbo fly. Because of air resistance, a bulky fly will be hard to cast, ruining the fluidity of fly casting and making work out of play. You will see how to incorporate fly tying materials that produce a simulation of sizable prey that is attractive to bass, but in fact won't hinder your ability to cast the fly.

Because bass prefer hefty food items such as fish smaller than themselves, crayfish, frogs, snakes, leeches, worms, and even baby ducks and birds, these flies are quite a contrast from traditional trout flies. Also, besides the conventional feathers, dubbing and deer hair, bass flies incorporate foam, cork, paint, plastic eyes, rubber legs, lead or non-toxic eyes, and special hooks. Instead of matching an insect hatch, you'll find yourself tying and fishing flies that resemble critters that eat insects, and in turn, are themselves prey for bass.

Tying Bass Flies attempts to give you all the information you need to tie these flies, but it can be very helpful if you watch a friend, fly club member, or a fly shop person tie these flies. Also, I list two helpful videos and special sources for supplies.

©1995 Deke Meyer
All Rights Reserved. No parts of this book may be reproduced without the written consent of the publisher, except in the case of brief excerpts in critical reviews and articles.

Published in 1995 by Frank Amato Publications, Inc.
PO Box 82112, Portland, Oregon 97282.

Cover photograph: Jim Schollmeyer
Book Layout: Alan Reid
Softbound ISBN: 1-57188-041-0
Printed in Hong Kong

1 3 5 7 9 10 8 6 4 2

TABLE OF CONTENTS

Tips for Preparing and Tying Materials

A supportive local fly club or shop is ideal and can prove to be a wealth of information. Mail order is workable if you get a knowledgeable salesperson.

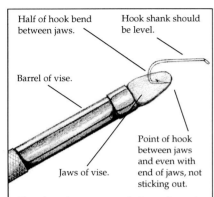

Half of hook bend between jaws.

Hook shank should be level.

Barrel of vise.

Point of hook between jaws and even with end of jaws, not sticking out.

Jaws of vise.

Fly tying vises vary greatly in quality, price, and types of clamping and adjustment. This illustration shows the proper placement of the hook in the jaws of the vise.

One of your first purchases will be a vise. If you're on a budget, I recommend buying an inexpensive one at first, then as you gain experience you will define your own preferences. You can use your first vise as a field kit vise or pass it on to another beginning tier.

Basic Bass Fly Tying Tools

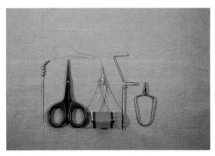

Besides a vise, basic tools needed for tying bass flies include: bobbin threader /cleaner, scissors, bobbin with thread, Matarelli Extended Reach Whip Finisher, and hackle pliers. (The Extended Reach Whip Finish tool is a must for the Wiggle Bug, and cork/foam poppers and sliders.)

Optional Tools

These tools will help you tie better bass bugs because they make it easier: heavy duty ceramic thread bobbin, rotating hackle pliers, Brassie hair packer, hair/hackle guard, hair stacker, bodkin /half hitch tool, heavy duty clippers.

How to Proceed: Tying the First Flies

The most important component in fly tying is the hook. You can tie and fish with inexpensive hooks but you will miss catching fish because the steel is too soft and the hook is usually dull. The best hooks are chemically sharpened—I recommend paying a little more and getting a whole lot more hook. After all, when you consider the amount of time and money you spend on tying flies, driving to the river or lake, and your investment in fly fishing gear, why scrimp when it comes to hooks?

To begin tying these flies, you need a package (of 25) of size 6 Stinger-type hooks, which are large gap, ring-eye hooks designed specifically for bass poppers, and a packet of 2X-long or 3X-long shank in size 6 for streamers. You can add more hooks later. You may want to consider nickel plated hooks, which are rust and saltwater resistant (for those fishing for bass in salty lagoons), available in some styles and sizes. Generally, flies used for largemouth are bigger than those for smallmouth bass; sizes 6 to 3/0 versus sizes 10 to 6. If you tie some size 8, 6 and 4 flies you can cover both species to begin with; you'll develop your own favorite styles and sizes of flies.

Start with either size A or 3/0 thread, which are strong enough to cinch down the materials without breaking the thread. The traditional color is black, which is fine, but many tiers match the thread to the body color of the fly. Start with a neutral color: tan, gray or pale olive. (Tiers who weight some of their flies with lead wire often tie the head with a specific color, such as red, to denote a weighted fly.) The easiest flies to tie are the Bass Woolly Bugger and the Deke's Bead Legs, followed by the Burk's Bass Flash. You can ease into the deer hair flies with the Henry's Crawfish; you can ease into the other poppers and sliders with those tied with soft foam bodies because you tie on the materials first, then add the body.

Before tying, mash the barb down on the hook with pliers. (If you accidentally break the hook, you won't forfeit an already tied fly.) Many quality waters are managed for catch-and-release fly fishing with barbless hooks, but just as important, if you stick your clothes or your anatomy with a hook, it will easily come out. Always wear some kind of eye protection—you can lose your sight to a fly hook.

It might seem complicated at first glance, but fly tying is simply a matter of practice and proportion. My first bass flies looked as if they had ejected from the vacuum cleaner, only to be stomped by indifferent feet. But I caught fish with those unruly

flies. With practice comes improvement, and fish eat imperfect flies.

I wish you enjoyable tying and fishing.

Bass Stinger Hooks

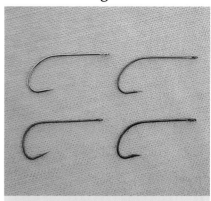

Tiemco 8089 nickel plated, size 10
Tiemco 8089, size 10
Daiichi 2720, size 3
Mustad 80300BR, size 10

The hooks above are the best currently-available, chemically sharpened stinger hooks designed specifically for bass. (You'll notice that hook shapes vary some, and size designations are not consistent between manufacturers.)

Attaching the Thread to the Hook

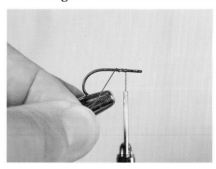

1) Hold end of thread between thumb and forefinger of left hand, wrap thread around hook shank with thread bobbin in right hand.

2) While maintaining light pressure on thread with thumb and forefinger with left hand, wrap thread back over itself with bobbin.

The Weedguard Option

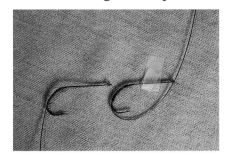

Because bass crave ambush cover, tie some of your flies with a weedguard. The loop style illustrated here is simple yet effective, using stiff monofilament about the same diameter as the hook wire (Maxima Chameleon 25# equals Mason 10# hard monofilament). The disadvantage of a weedguard is that it's also a fishguard, sometimes preventing the hook from penetrating the fish's mouth. So tie some of your flies without a weedguard, for fishing more open waters.

Step 1) Flatten the last 1/2 inch of the monofilament so the thread will hold it more securely. Attach thread, wrap back over mono, then forward to end of hook shank. (Thread goes down hook bend about 1/2 of distance to hook point.) Saturate with head cement or one drop of Zap-A-Gap cyanoacrylate super glue spread over thread with a toothpick. (If Zap-A-Gap is used, you can speed drying with an accelerator, but the fumes are nasty.)

Step 2) Tie in rest of materials; be sure to leave room for weedguard tie-down at head of fly.

Step 3) If the eye of the hook is large enough to accommodate the weedguard mono and the tippet monofilament, run the weedguard mono through the eye of the hook (as in the photo). If not, the weedguard mono must be laid either under the hook and just behind the hook eye, or alongside the shank and just behind the eye. The weedguard loop formed is wider than the hook gap by 1/2 to 1/4 the width of the hook gap.

Step 4) Secure the weedguard mono with thread tied right behind the hook eye.

Step 5) Clip off excess monofilament, leaving hook eye unobstructed. (Sharp sidecutter pliers or nail clippers may work better than your scissors—and saves the scissors for cutting less coarse materials.) Whip finish securely, cement well.

The Whip Finish

Using a Matarelli whip finish tool is highly recommended because it is quick and easy to use once you learn how, and the head on the fly will be small and tight, making your fly more durable. (These photos show the regular tool; for bass flies you need the Matarelli Extended Reach Whip Finish Tool.)

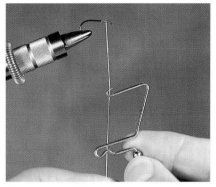

Step 1) Grasp the tool by the small ball at the top of the handle between thumb and forefinger of right hand, thread bobbin in left hand. Tool hook goes around thread; bottom bend stays on your side.

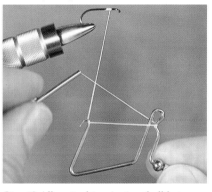

Step 2) Allow tool to pivot on ball between thumb and forefinger: thread forms triangle, from head of fly, through tool hook, around tool bend, then back across in front of thread from head of fly.

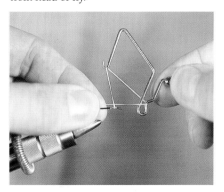

Step 3) Allow tool to pivot on ball again, flipping triangle upside down and bringing triangle above hook, maintaining light pressure on thread bobbin. (The tool bend stays on the right side while the tool hook flips out towards you, ending above the hook shank, but still in a triangle.)

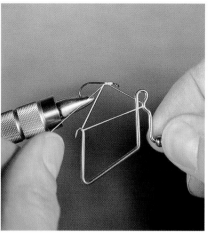

Step 4) Keeping tension on the thread and allowing the tool to pivot on the ball, keep the tool bend to the right and wrap thread around the hook shank with the tool hook three times. (You still have the triangle, the tool hook flips out towards you while the tool bend stays to the right.)

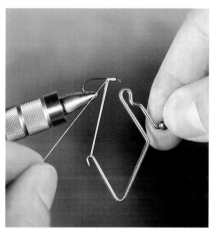

Step 5) Maintain pressure on the thread and on the tool hook, tip the tool bend down until the thread slips off, leaving thread attached to the head of the fly and the tool hook.

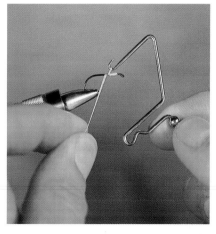

Step 6) Pull on the thread while sliding the tool hook up to the fly head.

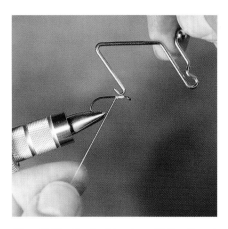

Step 7) Tip the tool hook until the thread slips off, tightening the thread, which finishes the whip finish. (Instead of wrapping thread around the fly head six times (Step 4) it's better to make two complete whip finishes of three wraps each. It makes a tighter head and if the first whip finish breaks you still have a usable fly and one you can later add another whip finish to.)

Preparing Pre-cut Cork and Hard Foam

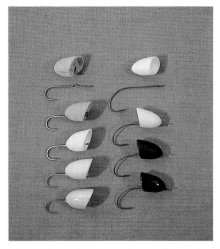

Step 1) The cork is probably already smooth. Smooth the hard foam with extra fine sandpaper or a nail file. Select a hook/head combination that allows enough hook shank length to tie on materials behind the head, and a large enough hook gap to hook bass. (The flat or cupped end forward for a popper; the pointed cone end forward for a slider.)

Step 2) Make sure slot cut on underside of head accommodates the hook shank. Mix epoxy and apply to hook slot with toothpick (don't use 5-minute epoxy, it dries too fast). Use extra epoxy to level the bottom of the head, covering the hook slot. (Large holes in cork head can be filled with epoxy.) If tying in optional weedguard, leave room behind the hook eye. Let dry overnight. Alternatively, use Zap-A-Gap or other super glue designed for porous materials. You can't fill in the hook slot, but you can begin painting right away. (The fastest is to super glue the white hard foam head, then just tie on the feathers, leaving the head white.)

Step 3) Cork needs a primer coat; hard foam does not. Either dip the head or brush on a coat of primer on the cork. After the first dries, sand smooth with extra fine sandpaper, then add another coat.

Step 4) After the primer dries, sand it smooth again. Paint the head in your desired color scheme. Some favorites include: frog (green on top, yellow on the bottom), black, white, red/white, yellow, yellow with black spots, and others. I prefer to paint the flat or cupped face of the popper white so I can see it better when I retrieve the fly. You will probably need to apply a second coat of paint after the first one dries. Enamel paints impart a glossier and tougher finish than acrylics, but the soap-and-water brush cleansing is less hassle than paint remover for enamels.

Step 5) After the final coat dries, either dip the head or paint on a coat of clear fixative to protect the paint. If you paint on eyes or use adhesive eyes, apply them before you put on the finish coat.

Preparing Deer Hair

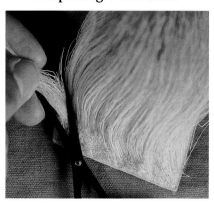

When you shop for deer hair, tell the salesperson that it's for tying bass bugs. Ideally, the hair should be about two inches long, springy and hollow, not found on all parts of the deer. Shops supply it in a variety of regular and fluorescent colors, such as natural, yellow, green, olive, black, white, chartreuse, gray, etc. When you're ready to tie with the hair, clip off about a pencil-thick bunch of hair.

Cleaning Deer Hair

Deer hair has a natural underfur that can collect water, which doesn't contribute to the floatation of a deer hair popper or slider. To remove the underfur, hold the deer hair by the tips, then brush it out with a comb or dog brush.

Stacking Deer Hair

After you've clipped off a pencil-thick bunch of hair and cleaned out the underfur, insert the hair tip-first into the stacker. Tap the stacker on a hard surface, which aligns the hair tips. Remove the hair from the stacker—the hair is now "stacked" so the tips are all even.

Tying Deer Hair—Banding

To get alternate color bands in your deer hair popper or slider, first tie in one color and spin it (as shown for Henry's Crawfish, page 22). Then tie in another color of deer hair and spin it, varying it to suit your color scheme.

After you trim the deer hair, the banding becomes more noticeable. It's debatable whether bass care or not, but banding looks pleasing to us, and the argument can be made that many creatures in nature, including some natural bass prey, exhibit banding in their coloration.

Tying Deer Hair— Contrasting Color

When tying deer hair bugs, many tiers prefer to simulate natural bass prey, such as frogs or snakes. These critters have light colored bellies and darker backs. The technique is similar for making the deer hair diving collar on the Dahlberg Diver, page 16. Spin on two separate clumps of the bottom color of deer hair, then back the thread up to the center of the two clumps. Hold a pencil-thick clump of the top color of hair above the hook, wrap two loose wraps of thread around the clump you're holding. Then pull straight down on the thread and the hair—don't spin it, just pin the hair down on top of the hook shank. Then move the thread forward, in front of all the hair you've tied in. Make an overhand knot around the shank and tighten the thread against the base of the deer hair to secure it (also called a granny knot, jam knot or half hitch). A half hitch tool is helpful.

The completed deer hair bug will show mottled coloration, with areas of darker color on top and extending down a little to the sides. It's debatable whether bass can see much of what the back of the fly looks like, but to us the contrasting colors look pretty snazzy. For example, the frog could have a white or yellow belly and a green or olive back. A snake could have a white belly and a brown back.

Pushing Deer Hair Tight

The deer hair bugs that float best are those that are tightly tied, with the deer hair compacted between tied in bunches of hair. One method for pushing the deer hair tight between clumps is to compact it with the ends of your thumb and fingers. Then make an overhand knot around the shank and tighten the thread against the base of the deer hair to secure it (also called a granny knot, jam knot or half hitch). A half hitch tool is helpful.

Another method for pushing the deer hair tight between clumps is to compact it with the Brassie, an inexpensive tool for compacting the hair. Then make an overhand knot around the shank and tighten the thread against the base of the deer hair to secure it.

Tying Off the Deer Hair Fly— The Hackle/Hair Guard

With all that deer hair sticking out around the eye of the hook, it can be difficult to whip finish the fly without entangling the deer hair in the thread. An inexpensive tool, the hackle/hair guard slips up over the thread and the eye of the hook, pinning the hair out of the way, allowing you to make a nice tight whip finish.

Flared Out Hackle Tips

You may want to add flared hackle tips to the tail. Chicken neck hackle has a natural curve, so you can tie it so it bends out away from the fly. When retrieved, the hackle slides in close to the body, but when you pause or stop the fly, the hackle "kicks out", making a lifelike scissoring action. Some tiers use flared out hackle tips to simulate the kicking action of frog legs. To get hackle that flares out to the side, select hackle from opposite halves of the neck, such as a feather from the left and one from the right side of the skin. You can tie them both in together, but it's easier to tie one in at a time.

Helpful Videos

"Tying Bass Flies With Jimmy Nix"
"Hooked On Fly Tying, Spinning Deer Hair With Chris Helm"

In addition to your local fly shop, keep these folks in mind:

For Soft Foam Bodies

EdgeWater
35 North 1000 West
Clearfield, UT 84015
(800) 584-7647
FAX (801) 825-0624

A Specialty Bass Fly Shop

The Bass Pond
PO Box 82
Littleton, CO 80160-0082
(800) 327-5014
FAX (303) 730-8932

Bass Woolly Bugger

HOOK:	2X-long, 3X-long or 4X-long shank, heavy wire, size 1/0-10
TAIL:	Marabou; Flashabou or Crystal Flash optional
BODY:	Yarn, chenille or dubbing
HACKLE:	Dyed wide saddle or neck hackle
EYES:	Optional, weighted barbell eyes
WEEDGUARD:	Optional, stiff monofilament, diameter matches hook diameter

The Woolly Bugger is an ideal underwater fly for bass because it simulates many prey items that bass like: baitfish, crayfish, dragonfly nymphs, leeches or other quarry. Also, the hackle and marabou creates the illusion of bulk and life-like movement, but without bulk. These materials collapse against the hook shank when cast, offering minimal air resistance and allowing for a smooth, streamlined cast.

Tying Tips

Some tie the Woolly Bugger without a lead wire underbody, theorizing that the fly swims more smoothly underwater and reacts better to the angler's fly line manipulations. The advantage to lead weighting is that the fly sinks better, and if you weight just the front of the fly as in the photos, the fly exhibits an up-and-down jigging effect on the retrieve, which attracts fish. The Woolly Bomber includes weighted eyes on the front of the fly. (Be sure to tie the eyes on top of the shank so the fly will flip over on the retrieve, helping to avoid snags.) There is no "right" or "wrong" way to tie this fly. Also, marabou "shrinks" when underwater, so tie in about twice the amount you want the sunken fly to display. However, too much marabou inhibits the sink rate of the fly.

Some good color combinations include (body/hackle): black/grizzly; black/olive; black/fluorescent blue with blue Flashabou in tail; brown/grizzly; brown/olive; brown/brown; all black, white or chartreuse.

Variations

The origins of the Woolly Bugger lie with the Woolly Worm. In *The Practical Fly Fisherman*, 1953, A.J. McClane wrote that the Woolly Worm "...made its reputation as an Ozark bass fly back in the 1920s. Actually this pattern was first described by Izaak Walton back in 1653 and has three centuries of recommendation to its credit."

If we look into one of the first written words on fly fishing, in *Treatise On Fysshynge Wiyh An Angle*, 1496, Juliana Berners wrote, "The wasp fly: the body of black wool and wound about with yellow thread, the wings of the buzzard." If we could view what Dame Berners tied, we might see a prototype black Woolly Worm with yellow thread rib and black palmered hackle. If not exactly what we use today, a black fly with loose flowing black hackle is an excellent prescription for a fish-catching fly, made all the better for the addition of a marabou tail.

Tie a few of these in various sizes, some with and some without a weedguard. To some, add a bit of Flashabou to the tail, to impart bright quick flashes that bass can see in turbid water.

Fishing Tips

A simple but effective technique is to cast close to cover, then retrieve the Bugger in quick 6-inch pulls of the line. Fishing a Bugger is exciting when bass smack the fly hard. Sometimes you may need to slow the retrieve, or even give it a jigging type of action, fishing it vertically as well as horizontally. Be alert for the light strike, and keep your rod pointed at the fly to better detect the strike and to get the maximum power into the hook set.

At other times you may need to retrieve the fly as fast as you can—simulating prey fleeing from the predator bass—but be sure to mount your fly on a stout tippet—the strike will be hard.

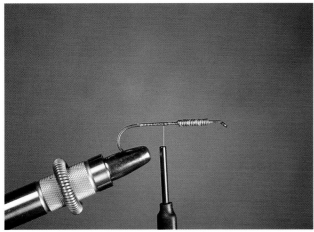

1) Debarb hook. Attach thread, wrap to rear of hook. Wrap lead wire around front half of hook, leaving room for head. (With your thumbnail mash the ends of the lead wire on the hook after wrapping, for a smooth thread and yarn transition.) Wrap thread forward through lead, then back to rear of lead wire. Cement thread and wire area.

2) Tie in marabou so it extends about hook shank length to the rear and butts up to the lead wire. (Tie in optional Flashabou or Crystal Flash if desired.) Trim excess and wrap enough thread to secure material. Cement well.

3) Move thread to the front of the body. Lay yarn on top of the body, wrap thread to rear of body, then up to the front.

4) Move thread back to tie in hackle by tip, shiny side forward, wet fly style. Leave room for at least one wrap of yarn behind hackle, in front of tail. (Hackle width should be about 1/2 hook shank length, with stubs left on trimmed hackle so thread will grip the stem better.)

5) Bring thread forward. Wrap yarn forward, tie off and trim. (Get one or two wraps of yarn between tail and hackle tie-in.) Cement yarn tie-down area.

6) Wrap hackle forward, tie off and trim excess. (If you desire more hackle at the front, tie in a front hackle, wrap it on, then tie it off. See Deke's Bead Legs, page 21, Steps 5 & 6.) Whip finish and cement head.

Burk's Bass Flash

Hook:	Stinger, sizes 2-10
Armature:	15# hard Mason monofilament; silver Flashabou
Sili Legs:	Lime with black specks (silicone legs)
Body:	Fluorescent red chenille butt; white chenille
Eyes:	Various weighted eyes: lead, nickel plate, non-toxic with pupil
Weedguard:	Mason hard monofilament, 15# for size 10, 20# for size 6, 25# for size 2

Designed by Andy Burk of Redding, California, this fly is his version of the spinner bait, the conventional gear combination of jig and spinner cluster that is deadly on bass. This fly incorporates more traditional fly tying materials in its Flashabou wing, chenille, silicone legs and weighted eyes.

Tying Tips

The fluorescent red chenille acts as a bit of colorful attractor, but this bit of chenille also locks the sili legs in place, making them radiate out from the fly. Andy mostly fishes size 10, but sometimes the larger sizes are more effective for early season bass.

Variations

You can tie this fly in other colors, but Andy says, "In looking in my friends' tackle boxes of conventional gear, the one color combination that really shined through was the chartreuse and silver. I've used black and orange and other combinations but the chartreuse and white is the one I keep coming back to because it works so consistently well." And whether the bass strike the fly because the silver flash simulates a wounded baitfish or because the bass are aggravated into attacking an intruder, this fly works.

You can substitute another stiff monofilament for Mason hard mono in the armature, such as Maxima Chameleon, but for stiffness, Mason hard 15# equals Maxima 25#.

Fishing Tips

The Burk's Bass Flash is versatile: you can fish it on a floating or sinking line and vary your tactics. Andy says, "My favorite type of water to fish it is among fallen timber. Closely watch the fly line as the fly sinks. A lot of times the fish hammer it as it sinks into their lair. You can swim it back past a tree trunk or cast it right up against the shoreline and swim it back.

"When you look at how spinner baits are fished by conventional fishermen, they're fished extremely fast. On a floating line in shallow water, particularly with fallen timber or along a steep drop-off bank, I'll let the fly fall, and then begin a fairly fast retrieve, with 2-foot pulls. If I hold the rod high, I can make it "V" along the surface, just like a spinner bait.

"With a sinking line, I'll cast the fly out on a short leader (4-6 feet), make sure the line is straight, hold the rod tip low, with the line over my finger, and I watch very carefully as the fly sinks. A lot of times the fish will hit it as the fly falls. I start with fast 4 to 6 inch pulls, then just steady, long pulls that bounce the fly off cover and the bottom contours. This fly has that seductive appearance, and even when you stop moving the fly, the fly is still moving because those silicone legs will not pause—they are always in motion."

This is certainly not the typical bass popper, but if you tie the Burk's Bass Flash and put it front of a bass, you may motivate them into motion, too.

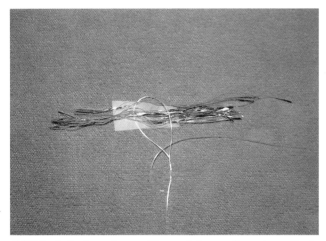

1) With six inches of monofilament, form a three-turn clinch knot around 25 strands of Flashabou three inches long. (Moistening your fingers and then stroking the Flashabou makes it easier to handle.)

2) Tighten clinch knot around Flashabou, trim excess monofilament from knot. Apply one drop of super glue to knot.

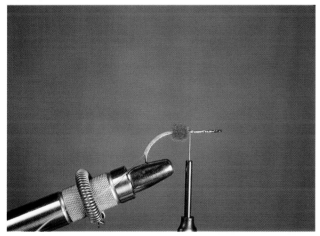

3) Insert debarbed hook in vise, attach thread, tie in weedguard, cement thread. Tie in fluorescent red chenille after stripping the chenille from its core, pulling it between your thumbnail and first finger, to give small tie-in area. (Take a peek at photo for Step 5 to see how white chenille core is tied on.) Wrap as butt, tie off and trim excess. Cement tie-down area.

4) Tie down eyes securely and about 20 sili legs (for size 10 fly). Cement tie-down area.

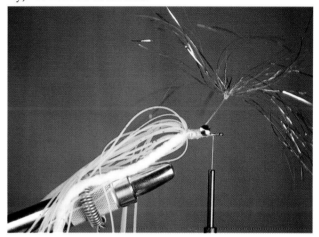

5) Tie in Flashabou armature with it extending about 3/4 inch above the fly (with Flashabou trimmed to one inch). Armature will extend up from just behind the eyes. (It helps to bend the mono with pliers.) Trim excess mono. Tie in white chenille core. Wrap thread forward and cement tie-down area.

6) Wrap white chenille forward, tight against sili legs and locking armature in upright position. You may want to criss-cross chenille over eyes tie-down area (be sure to leave room to tie off weedguard). Tie in weedguard, trim excess, whip finish and cement head. Trim legs to about hook shank length behind hook.

Cork/Hard Foam Popper

Hook:	Stinger, size 3/0 to 10
Tail:	Marabou, hackle tips, Crystal Flash optional
Hackle:	Dyed or natural chicken hackle
Rubber Legs:	White or various colors, round or flat
Body:	Cork or hard foam, flat or cupped end forward
Eyes:	Optional, painted, adhesive or doll eyes
Weedguard:	Optional, stiff monofilament, diameter matches hook diameter

In his *Book of the Black Bass*, 1881, 1923, James Henshall wrote, "The first bass bugs that I remember were made and sent to me during the World's Fair at Chicago, 1893. They were made from plump, buoyant bodies, dressed with silk floss and feathers, and with long wings, hackles, tails, and streamers of prismatic hues." He quoted a letter from B.F. Wilder:

"In 1911, Mr. Louis Adams of New York gave me a cork bug, tied by himself or to his order. It was extremely attractive, but due to faults in construction it was hard to hook the fish that struck it.

"During that summer I improved the bug. I changed the shape and balance of the body, thus making it always float with the hook down, and I securely anchored the hook in the cork body by means of a sheet-steel fin soldered on the hook-shank. The resulting bug was as attractive as those tied by Mr. Adams, and it was now possible to hook the greater portion of the striking fish. But the changes I made were only improvements; Mr. Adams was the inventor.

"In 1912 I used this cork bug in Maine and taught Mr. James True of Norway, Maine, how to tie it. During 1913 he made and sold hundreds of bugs."

Historically, the first cork flies consisted of feathers or hair strapped onto cork with lashings of thread. Interestingly enough, no difference was drawn between flat face or cone face cork flies. Poppers or sliders were not mentioned, they were all just called bugs.

Tying Tips

As with the cork/hard foam slider, I find it best to prepare a batch of popper heads beforehand, then tying the rest of the fly when the glue and paint have properly hardened. (For steps in preparing cork or hard foam, see page 6.) For better visibility on the retrieve, I prefer to leave the white hard foam face as is, or paint the cork face white.

The advantage of hard foam is that you don't need to fill gaps in the body, as you might with cork, and hard foam doesn't require a primer coat. The advantage to using epoxy (don't use 5-minute epoxy because it sets up too fast) is that you can fill the slot for the hook with glue; with Zap-A-Gap or other porous-type super glue the advantage is that the fly body doesn't need to sit very long—you can begin painting the body the same day.

Variations

The most important variation is the pencil popper, in either hard foam or cork. A pencil popper is the soul of simplicity, just an elongated body with a tail of marabou and Crystal Flash. Some fisher folks surmise that a pencil popper simulates a wounded or floundering baitfish, an irresistible mouthful for bass.

When creating poppers, go for variety in color and size, because bass may prefer a large or small popper, and water clarity and amount of sunlight on the water play a part in a popper's success. Some standard bass colors are white, white/red, black, yellow, yellow/black, chartreuse, and green/yellow as a froggie simulator.

Fishing Tips

Since cork is more dense it sits lower in the water; when you fish your poppers, you'll find that cork moves more water on the "pop" than hard foam.

Try popping your bug lightly at first, because a loud pop may scare fish instead of making them want to eat your bug. Most people fish poppers too fast; start slow and intersperse your retrieve with pauses—give the bass a chance to react to your fly. Also, don't just hammer one cast into a spot and move on; make several presentations to the same spot—each time you do, you pull on the bass's strike trigger and increase your chances at a hook-up. Catching a bass on a topwater popper is one of the joys of fly fishing. Go ahead and try it—the "pop, pop, pop" of the retrieve is relaxing, and bass just love to blast a popper.

1) Hook with cork should already be debarbed. Attach thread, wrap hook shank with thread, then cement. Tie on marabou (hook shank length) and optional Crystal Flash. Trim excess and cement.

4) Wrap hackle around hook shank, tie off. Trim excess and cement.

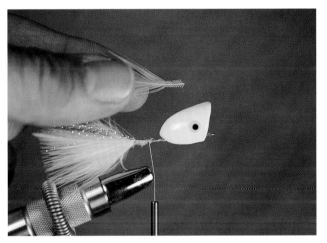

2) Tie in optional flared hackle tips (which flare to the outside), with stubs left on trimmed hackle so thread will grip the stem better, keeping them fairly even with hook shank. Secure well with thread and cement. (You can tie them both in together, but it's easier to tie one in at a time.)

5) Put overhand knot in rubber legs (3), slip over body to tie-down area. Wrap over with thread.

3) Tie in optional collar hackle (width equals hook gap), with stubs left on trimmed hackle so thread will grip the stem better.

6) Whip finish and cement. Trim legs to about hook shank length.

Cork/Hard Foam Slider

Hook:	Stinger, size 3/0 to 10
Tail:	Marabou, hackle tips, Crystal Flash optional
Hackle:	Dyed or natural chicken hackle
Rubber Legs:	White or various colors, round or flat
Body:	Cork or hard foam, rounded end forward
Eyes:	Optional, painted or glass eyes
Weedguard:	Optional, stiff monofilament, diameter matches hook diameter

In his *Book of the Black Bass*, 1881, 1923, James Henshall included a color plate with three Wilder Feather Minnows. He quoted an article written in 1921 by B.F. Wilder: "I hit upon a head made of cork and a body composed of long, springy cock hackles. These feathers were tied in on either side of the hook-shank with the natural curve of the feathers of one side opposed to the curve of those forming the other side, which resulted in a very flexible body with the appearance of substance and of almost no weight. When the completed lure floated in its testing vessel it floated barely awash; it appeared to struggle helplessly at the slightest movement of the leader."

Although constructed with the cone shaped head we would call a slider, the Feather Minnows were grouped under the general term of "bugs". And even though the cork or hard foam popper is the most commonly used topwater fly for bass, don't overlook the cork or hard foam slider. Because bass are often hooked on cork poppers, they soon learn to avoid them, and the biggest bass learn the quickest and remember the longest.

The slider merely slips underwater, sometimes with a slight gurgling sound, swimming along without fish-scaring noise, seducing bass with its quiet demeanor. When bass are in the shallows and it's windy, a slider often works better than a popper because the slider spends much of its time just under the surface where the bass can see it. The popping noise of the popper is lost in the wave and wind disturbance.

Tying Tips

As with the cork or hard foam popper, I find it best to prepare a batch of slider heads beforehand, then tying the rest of the fly when the glue and paint have properly hardened. (For steps in preparing cork or hard foam, see page 12.)

Variations

As you shop for slider heads, you will find that their shapes vary with suppliers, and that some shapes are only available in either cork or hard foam, but not both. Also, cork is more dense, so when fishing, it has a slightly different action on the retrieve. Although you will undoubtedly discover your favorites, the advantage to trying various slider shapes and sizes is that they respond differently when you retrieve them through bass water. Some silently slip, some splash a little, and some gurgle. You may develop preferences for sizes and "action" for sliding sliders in front of bass.

You may want to add flared hackle tips to the tail. To get hackle that flares out to the side, select hackle from opposite halves of the neck, such as a feather from the left and one from the right side of the skin. You can tie them both in together, but it's easier to tie one in at a time.

Traditionally, flat white rubber legs were used, but I prefer the round rubber legs. Although available in various colors, white remains a favorite.

Fishing Tips

Try varying your retrieve with the slider, keeping it under the surface for much of the time, giving the bass plenty of time to see the fly. Also, don't be in a hurry to cast to a new spot. Swim your slider by each likely spot at least three times—each pass through pulls just that much more at the bass's strike trigger. The final retrieve may be just enough to send the bass into strike mode, shooting out to nail your slider.

1) Hook with cork or hard foam should already be debarbed. Attach thread, wrap hook shank with thread, then cement. Tie in weedguard. Tie on marabou (hook shank length) and optional Crystal Flash. Trim excess and cement.

2) Tie in optional flared hackle tips (which flare to the outside), with stubs left on trimmed hackle so thread will grip the stem better, keeping them fairly even with hook shank. (See Soft Foam Popper, Step 2, page 27.) Secure well with thread and cement. (You can tie them in both together, but it's easier to tie one in at a time.)

3) Tie in optional collar hackle (width equals hook gap), with stubs left on trimmed hackle so thread will grip the stem better. (See Soft Foam Slider, Step 3, page 29.) You may need a second hackle.

4) Wrap hackle around hook shank, tie off. Trim excess, whip finish and cement.

5) Put rubber leg in eye of needle. Press needle with folded leg through cork/hard foam with vise grips or pliers. (With large needle you can install more than one doubled-up leg at a time.) When legs get almost through body, put one drop of super glue on legs so they will be cemented inside the body.

6) Re-attach thread at eye. Tie off weedguard, cut excess, whip finish and cement. Glue on optional eyes.

Dahlberg Diver

Hook:	Stinger, sizes 3/0-10
Tail:	Marabou, Flashabou or Crystal Flash
Hackle:	Hackle tips, flared out, in the tail
Collar:	Hackle
Rubber Legs:	Optional, varied colors, round or flat
Body Collar:	Deer hair (can stiffen with silicone adhesive)
Body:	Deer Hair
Eyes:	Optional, solid glass
Weedguard:	Stiff monofilament matched to hook size

Larry Dahlberg of Brainerd, Minnesota told me he first developed his diver in 1977 when he was 18 years old. He says, "I had a particular fish I was trying to catch, a big bass, and I wanted to catch it on a fly rod. It was in the spring and the bass would follow poppers all the time. I wanted to get something that would dive under the water and swim back up. I changed the shape of the deer hair to make the fly do what it needed to do."

That bass weighed 6 pounds 7 ounces; the Dahlberg Diver has since tricked boxcar loads of bass and other predator species, as well as spawning countless variations of the original Dahlberg Diver design. And although originally conceived for largemouth, this diver is deadly on smallmouth as well.

Tying Tips

There is no standard color pattern for this fly; you can't go wrong with black, purple, yellow, white, chartreuse or chocolate brown. You can mix and vary materials and colors of your own choosing, as some tiers do when they tie divers to mimic baitfish, frogs or other bass prey. It's a good idea to carry divers in various colors and sizes, because bass tend to have minds of their own about what they want to eat. Water clarity is also a factor.

You can vary the steepness of the fly's dive on the retrieve by the varying the height and stiffness of the deer hair collar, or by applying silicone adhesive to the collar. George Harmeling of Memphis, Tennessee ties some of his divers with small lead eyes under the head of the fly, increasing the dive rate.

Generally, the nose of the fly is tied small, in a cone shape, so the fly will begin digging down into the water. Because the fly dives, and often encounters subsurface snags you can't see, it's most often tied with a weedguard.

Variations

One of the most effective variations of the first design was to substitute a rabbit strip tail for the marabou and hackle tips. One of the keys to the effectiveness of the deer hair diving collar is that it changes the water flow around the fly. When you retrieve the fly, or when it's swimming in moving water, the collar creates a vortex, a space behind the collar that allows for a bubble chain of oxygen bubbles. That attracts fish and makes the fly seem alive. Also, the rabbit strip tail tends to kick around in that bubble chain, further enhancing the effectiveness of this fly.

Fishing Tips

The Dahlberg Diver is most often fished with a floating line, and that works well, too. An equally effective tactic is to fish this diver with a sinktip line with a fast-sinking 5 feet tip. (A 10 foot tip is too long to be effective.) The leader should be 3 to 4 feet long.

You cast the fly, then allow time for the line to sink. When you pull on the line, the fly follows the sunken tip downward, diving in a steeper plane than with the floater. The fly will attain more depth on the retrieve, yet when you stop the retrieve, this deer hair fly will attempt to rise to the surface. You let it rise a bit, then pull it again. This up-and-down swimming action is deadly on bass; in fact, you might call this fly the Deadly Dahlberg Diver.

1) Debarb hook, insert in vise. Attach thread. (Tie in optional weedguard, see page 4.) Tie in marabou tail, optional Flashabou or Crystal Flash. Tie in flared-out hackle tips. (For trimming detail, see Foam Popper, Step 2, page 27.) Cement tie-down area.

2) Tie in hackle for collar, and wrap around hook shank. Trim excess and cement. (For more detail, see Foam Popper, Steps 3 & 4, page 27.)

3) Clean and stack a pencil-thick bunch of deer hair. Wrap two loose turns (while holding hair), tips to the rear. Release hair while pulling straight down on thread. As hair flares around hook, wrap one tight turn of thread around hair. Stroke hair back to the rear, bring thread forward through hair, wrap one turn around hook shank in front of hair. Push hair back with hair pusher tool or ends of fingers. Make an overhand or granny knot (called half hitch) with thread around hook shank, push tight up against hair and tighten knot. Wrap thread 1/4 inch ahead of hair. (See Henry's Crawfish, Steps 2 & 3, page 23). Spin on a second clump of hair, but do not wrap thread forward.

4) Add another clump of hair for the diving collar, but don't spin it. Tie in a pencil-thick bunch of hair by pulling straight down on the thread (but don't spin it). Pull hair up and back, and wrap thread forward.

5) Fill remainder of hook shank with spun deer hair, but leave room for the head (and optional weedguard). Whip finish and cement. (A hackle guard helps, see page 7.)

6) Take fly out of vise and trim hair, leaving collar (which can be stiffened with silicone adhesive). (Tie off optional weedguard, see page 4.) Use silicone adhesive to attach optional eyes. (Fly is in vise for photo.)

Deer Hair Popper

Hook:	Stinger, 3/0-10
Tail:	Marabou, optional Flashabou or Crystal Flash, flared hackle tips
Hackle:	Collar, various colors
Collar:	Deer hair tips
Rubber Legs:	White or various colors, round or flat
Body:	Spun and trimmed deer hair
Eyes:	Doll eyes
Weedguard:	Optional, matches hook size

The first bass poppers and sliders were made from wood or cork around the turn of the century. Before long, bass bugs were also tied with deer hair. Orley Tuttle created one of the first commercially available deer hair bugs, the Tuttle's Devil Bass Bug. In 1922, the Tuttles were marketing some 50,000 Devil Bugs in 800 different models and styles. Of course, one reason for their success is that bass love deer hair poppers.

It's not clear whether bass hit poppers because they think it's a fish or frog struggling to escape or it's just frightened prey. Maybe it's because bass are predators; if it looks alive and a bass can get it into its capacious mouth, a bass will attack it.

Tying Tips

When shopping for deer hair for bass bugs, be sure to specify that you want hair that spins good popper bodies. Good hair will be long and hollow, and is dyed in a number of subtle and gaudy fluorescent colors. You will develop your own preferences, but some favorites are black, white, frog, red/white, black/purple, chartreuse, yellow, olive, gray and others.

When you tie in the last clump of hair, use white. When you retrieve the fly, that bit of white in front will increase the fly's visibility. When the bass takes the fly in a quick boil, which they sometimes do, you can see the strike, particularly in low light conditions or when the fly is in the shade of an overhanging tree, a prime bass spot.

After trimming it, you can use silicone adhesive on the deer hair in front to firm up the popper face, allowing for a crisper "pop" on the retrieve. You can also put it on the bottom to help strengthen the fly (it keeps the deer hair from twisting).

Variations

You should carry deer hair poppers in a variety of colors and sizes. Sometimes the bass will show a preference for a color, or you may need a bright fly on an overcast day or towards dark. The smaller size poppers are nice for using with a light rod.

The most important variation is the deer hair slider, tied with a cone shaped face. The slider eases through the water, not spooking fish or alerting hard-fished bass that it's a popper. Sliders are especially effective when it's so windy that the bass can't hear or see the popper. The slider slips underwater, allowing the bass to see it more clearly.

Fishing Tips

Because the clipped deer hair will eventually soak up water, you need to dress the popper body with some type of silicone fly floatant. Don't get any on the tail or hackle because you want that part of the popper to undulate under the water.

When fishing a popper, vary your retrieve. Slow is often the best, interspersed with pauses. I prefer modest little pops at first, with pauses, only graduating to more vigorous pops when I'm convinced that the fish want loud, boisterous pops. When slow doesn't work, try faster and faster retrieves until your fly is popping and skipping across the water.

Bass will often hit a popper they think is "getting away", chasing it down as a predator after prey. Initially, though, most fly flingers fish their topwater flies too fast and loud, ripping the fly off the water just about the time the bass decides to strike the fly. Whether slow or fast, you'll find that bass love to attack a deer hair popper, made all the more fun because you tied it.

18

1) Debarb hook, insert in vise. Attach thread. (Tie in optional weedguard, see page 4.) Tie in marabou tail, optional Flashabou or Crystal Flash. Tie in flared-out hackle tips. (For trimming detail, see Foam Popper, Step 2, page 27.) Cement tie-down area.

2) Tie in hackle for collar, and wrap around hook shank. Trim excess and cement. (For more detail, see Foam Popper, Steps 3 & 4, page 27.)

3) Clean and stack a pencil-thick bunch of deer hair. Wrap two loose turns (while holding hair), tips to the rear. Release hair while pulling straight down on thread. As hair flares around hook, wrap one tight turn of thread around hair. Stroke hair back to the rear, bring thread forward through hair, wrap one turn around hook shank in front of hair. Push hair back with hair pusher tool or ends of fingers. Make an overhand or granny knot (called half hitch) with thread around hook shank, push tight up against hair and tighten knot. (Add second clump of hair if necessary.) Wrap thread 1/4 inch ahead of hair. (See Henry's Crawfish, Steps 2 & 3, page 23).

4) Tie in a second clump of hair. Make an overhand or granny knot in the rubber leg material and slip it over the shank of the hook. (See Cork Popper, Step 5, page 13.) Press the rubber up against hair and wrap one turn of thread over it and cement it. (Don't trim legs now; it helps to use a vise spring to keep the legs out of the way.)

5) Tie in more deer hair and rubber legs, leaving room for the head and optional weedguard tie-down. (For optional color banding or added spots of color, see page 6.) Whip finish and cement. (A hackle guard helps, see page 7.)

6) Remove fly from vise. Trim hair (except collar tips) to popper shape, flat top, bottom and face. With scissors or wood burning tool, make indentations in hair for doll eyes. Use silicone adhesive to attach eyes (and reinforce the face and bottom of the deer hair body). (Tie off optional weedguard, see page 4.)

Deke's Bead Legs

Hook:	2X or 3X-long shank, heavy wire, sizes 1/0-10
Tail:	Marabou; Crystal Flash or Flashabou optional
Body:	Yarn, various colors
Rubber Legs:	Round, white
Hackle:	Can match or contrast with body color
Bead:	Sized to hook size, gold or nickel
Weedguard:	Optional, stiff monofilament, diameter matches hook diameter

A variation of the Woolly Bugger, this fly incorporates a bead head for a jigging action on the retrieve and a bit of light reflective sparkle, and round rubber legs that fish find so enticing. Soft, flexible marabou tail and front hackle react seductively to your fly line machinations, teasing fish to strike. This fly design has this potential for lifelike movement, but the materials collapse against the hook shank when cast, so the fly is easy to cast. It imparts the impression of bulky prey without being bulky.

The rubber legs are locked into the body of the fly by thread and the yarn, so the legs won't come loose. Unlike square rubber legs, round legs won't fold up against the body of the fly or clump together, but undulate like bass-luring antennae. The round rubber legs vibrate with the slightest of nudges you impart to the fly. When the fly brushes against underwater structure the legs bend and then spring out when free of the structure—an elastic life-like movement fish can't resist.

Tying Tips

You can wrap lead wire at the head of the fly for a more pronounced jigging effect. The weight-forward design puts extra "kick" in the marabou tail. When you employ a bottom-bouncing retrieve, the nose of Deke's Bead Legs thumps along the bottom; when largemouth feel those vibrations via nerves in their inner ear and lateral line, it signals prey and they attack.

If you use a countersunk bead, put the wider part to the rear to better accommodate the end of the mono weedguard or the extra bulk of the lead wire. When working with Flashabou or Crystal Flash, it helps to moisten your finger tips, then stroke the material; it won't flare out when you handle it.

Some good color combinations include (body/hackle): black/grizzly; black/olive; black/fluorescent blue with blue Flashabou in tail; brown/grizzly; brown/olive; brown/brown; all black, white or chartreuse.

Variations

Some feel a Woolly Bugger style fly isn't properly dressed without Crystal Flash or Flashabou in the tail. With its quality of subtlety, Crystal Flash is appropriate in clear water conditions. Flashabou endows more intense reflective flash, helpful in turbid water that is common to bass swamps. (Electric blue is my favorite, with purple or black marabou.)

Fishing Tips

For largemouth bass I tie some with weedguards and some without. Cartoonist Gene Trump calls them fishguards because just as that stiff monofilament impedes hook penetration in snags it also impedes hook penetration in fish. For heavy cover a weedguard may be mandatory; for open areas or for retrieving your fly along structure but not through it, a weedguard is not necessary. When fishing subsurface, bass often inhale the fly with a mouthful of water while swimming in the same direction as the retrieve. A fly sans weedguard increases your hookup percentage when the strike is transmitted as just a subtle twitch in the fly line. For imparting maximum fly response to your fly rod and line manipulations, use an open loop knot or metal snap to attach the fly to the tippet. The Deke's Bead Legs is an excellent fly to draw a bead on a big bass—but be sure to use a stout tippet—when that big bass takes the fly it will surely dive for snaggy cover.

1) Debarb hook, slide bead onto hook. (A drop of Zap-A-Gap cyanoacrylate super glue will hold the bead in place, out of the way.) Install hook in vise. (Tie in optional weedguard if desired.) Tie in marabou tail, about hook shank length. (Tie in optional Flashabou or Crystal Flash, if desired.) Saturate tie-down with head cement.

2) Tie in two pair of rubber legs each side (four legs sprout from each side). Leave room between legs for secure tie-down and body material. (Wait until the fly is finished to trim the legs. Leave room at the front for hackle.) To keep the marabou tail out of the way, moisten your finger tips and stroke the marabou to the rear. (A spring mounted on your vise helps to hold the first set of legs out of the way when you tie in the second set.)

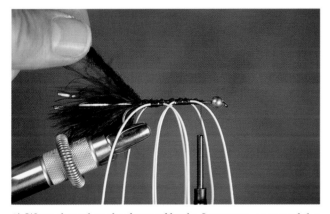

3) Wrap thread to the front of body. Lay yarn on top of the body, (leave room for hackle), tie down yarn by wrapping thread back towards tail, then forward to front of body. (A needle or bodkin is helpful for steering the thread around the legs.)

4) Wrap yarn forward to form body, allowing legs to stick straight out. Tie off yarn and trim excess. Cement tie-down area.

5) Tie in front hackle, shiny side facing forward, wet fly style. Hackle width should be about 1/2 hook shank length, with stubs left on trimmed hackle so thread will grip the stem better.

6) Wrap hackle around hook with hackle pliers, tie off, trim excess hackle. (Insert end of optional weedguard into bead after adjusting length of guard, tie down guard.) Whip finish head and cement. Trim legs to about hook shank length.

Henry's Crawfish

Hook:	2X or 3X-long shank, heavy wire, sizes 4-10
Tail:	Natural deer hair
Hackle:	Optional, brown
Body:	Natural deer hair
Eyes:	Lead barbell, or other weighted eyes
Weedguard:	Optional

I was introduced to this fly by Chip Hall at Gillionville Plantation, Albany, Georgia. Chip's version was a take-off of a bonefish fly by Tim Borski of Islamorada, Florida, but this final crawfish is a simplified rendition by Henry Williamson. Henry is a fly fishing instructor from northern Georgia with an eye towards designing flies that are easy to tie and catch fish.

This crayfish pattern is simple, but deadly for large-mouth and smallmouth bass, and for any fish that eat cray-fish. The mottled effect of natural deer hair mimics the broken camouflage of natural crayfish; when crayfish swim, their claws are swept straight back behind them, as suggested by the deer hair tail. Also, when bass bite this fly, the deer hair is kind of crunchy, just as the natural crayfish must be, so bass tend to hold onto the fly long enough for you to set the hook.

Tying Tips

Don't try to make a work of art when tying this fly; it's designed to be a rough approximation of a baby crayfish, and as such, don't sweat the artistic dignity of this fly. You can enjoy the skill of fly tying when you're extricating the fly from the mouth of a husky bass. Henry's Crawfish is meant to be fished, and is most effective in the smaller sizes.

Variations

You can add a palmered body hackle to this fly, but it's really not necessary. The lead eyes are tied on top of the hook, so when fished, the fly swims upside down, keeping the hook point up away from snags, making a weedguard unnecessary. Because the underwater take to this fly is often light, and because the fly is so easy and inexpensive to tie, it makes sense to just tie up a bunch of them, without worrying about a weedguard. A weedguard is often a fishguard that makes hooking fish more difficult.

Fishing Tips

A floating line is fine for fishing this fly. You ease it back to you in short, smooth strips on the retrieve. You are mimicking the swim-and-pause progress of a baby crayfish that is just foolish enough to dare a bass to strike. With weighted eyes you can get down five feet in still water, but if you need to get deeper you can add micro-shot or go with a sinktip or full sinking line.

The average lifespan for crayfish is two years, so they survive by being prolific. Crayfish bear young in the spring, summer and fall months, so baby crayfish are prey to bass all year. Studies by biologists have proven that crayfish are a favorite largemouth and smallmouth bass food. Since crayfish are common throughout the U.S., this fly is effective wherever bass swim. When bass won't move to the top to take your popper, try going down to them, presenting the bass with a menu item they can't refuse—a baby crayfish.

I have to agree with Chip Hall's assessment of Henry's Crawfish: "This fly is the greatest thing since grits."

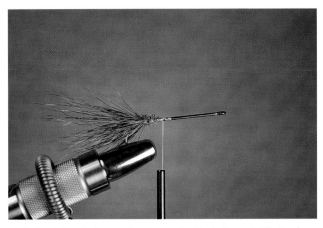

1) Debarb hook, insert in vise and attach thread. Tie in deer hair tail, length equals hook shank. (Don't worry about making the hair ends even, since crawfish claws are unruly, we are merely suggesting them.) Trim excess hair where tied down.

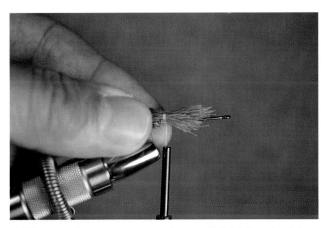

2) Wrap two loose turns around a pencil-thick bunch of deer hair and hook shank (while holding hair).

3) Release hair while pulling straight down on thread. As hair flares around hook, wrap one tight turn of thread around hair. Stroke hair back to the rear, bring thread forward through hair, wrap one turn around hook shank in front of hair. Push hair back with hair pusher tool or ends of fingers. Make an overhand or granny knot (called half hitch) with thread around hook shank, push tight up against hair and tighten knot. (A hatch hitch tool is helpful.) Wrap thread 1/4 inch ahead of hair.

4) Repeat Step 3 until hook shank covered, but leave room for the eyes and whip finished head.

5) Tie down barbell eyes on top of hook securely, whip finish and cement head.

6) Trim hair flat on top and bottom and as wide as the eyes. (Don't worry about it too much. Fly is in the vise for the photo; it's easier to trim the fly out of the vise.)

Rabbit Strip Slider

Hook:	Stinger, 3/0-10
Tail:	Rabbit strip
Hackle:	Deer hair tips as a collar
Rubber Legs:	Optional, various colors, round or flat
Body:	Deer hair
Eyes:	Optional, doll eyes
Weedguard:	Optional, matches hook size

There are two basic styles of rabbit strip fly. One is the Dahlberg Diver style, designed to dive, with the rabbit strip wiggling in its wake. The other style is similar to a slider, slithering along, but with a long rabbit tail. The rabbit strip excites bass because it moves so well on the retrieve, yet also dangles when the fly is still.

Randy Sublett of Mountain Home, Arkansas ties his Sneaky Snake rabbit strip fly in dark brown with a white belly. Jack Ellis of Woodville, Texas ties his favorite, the Grinnel Fly, in natural, black, or olive. Mark Sturtevant of Scotland, Pennsylvania ties his Fire Tiger in a combination of fluorescent chartreuse, fluorescent orange and black. This rabbit strip approach appeals to many creative tiers, and I'm sure it will attract you, as well.

Tying Tips

You can vary the color scheme of this fly to suit your fancy; some good colors include white, black, chartreuse, natural, olive, and others. You can add Flashabou or Crystal Flash, marabou in various colors, a hackle collar, and rubber legs.

When shopping for rabbit strips, try to get the thinnest you can find, but are still fully covered with hair. The wider strips don't attract any more bass, but because the hide soaks up water and becomes heavy, the wide strip rabbit is a hindrance to cast. The advantage to thin strips is that you still get all that bass-attracting movement, but without bulk. That's what makes fly fishing for bass so much fun—fishing with flies that simulate bulk to attract bass, but are actually light and easy to cast, especially on a light rod.

Variations

The larger the deer hair head, the more buoyant the fly will be. You can also add buoyancy with large doll eyes. If you want a fly that floats lower in the surface film, or you want to toss your fly on a light rod, make the deer head fairly small.

My favorite variation is to tie the rabbit strip fly with a foam head. You can use a hard or soft foam slider head, (just as you would with a cork or foam slider), but I prefer the soft foam EdgeWater diver head. It has more slant, causing the fly to dive some on the retrieve. The EdgeWater diver head comes with eye holes already drilled out, so you can install glass eyes with stems, or lead eyes, which increase the dive rate (but also make the fly harder to cast).

Fishing Tips

The Rabbit Strip Slider design is meant to be fished in and around cover, fairly slowly, to give the rabbit a chance to undulate in front of the bass. We can speculate that the long tail mimics worms or snakes, both of which bass eat. This design is particularly effective on hard-fished waters where bass often see poppers, in clear water where bass can see the rabbit strip from a long ways off, and in windy conditions where a popper is less effective.

One of my favorite tactics is the rabbit strip "Hang Down". I glide the fly up alongside or in bass cover, then just let the fly sit. The water-soaked rabbit will hang down below the surface, dangling and slightly wiggling, looking very much alive to the hungry bass. Be sure to mount a stout tippet—the Rabbit Strip Slider will strip bass of any doubt—they will lance out of cover and attack your fly.

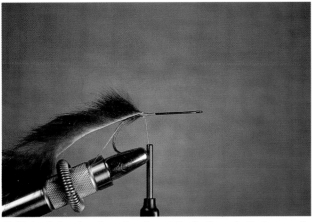

1) Debarb hook, place in vise. Attach thread, tie in weedguard. Tie in rabbit tail securely and cement (about 3 inches long, 1/8 inch wide).

2) Clean and stack a pencil-thick bunch of deer hair. Wrap two loose turns (while holding hair), tips to the rear.

3) Release hair while pulling straight down on thread. As hair flares around hook, wrap one tight turn of thread around hair. Stroke hair back to the rear, bring thread forward through hair, wrap one turn around hook shank in front of hair. Push hair back with hair pusher tool or ends of fingers. Make an overhand or granny knot (called half hitch) with thread around hook shank, push tight up against hair and tighten knot. (Add second clump of hair if necessary.) Wrap thread 1/4 inch ahead of hair. (See Henry's Crawfish, Steps 2 & 3, page 23).

4) Repeat Step 3 until hook shank covered, but leave room for the weedguard and whip finished head.

5) Remove fly from vise. Trim hair (except collar tips) to cone shape. With scissors or wood burning tool, make indentations in hair for doll eyes. Use silicone adhesive to attach eyes.

6) Install fly in vise, re-attach thread. Adjust weedguard loop, tie down securely, clip excess monofilament. (See page 4.) Whip finish and cement. (A hackle guard helps, see page 7.)

Soft Foam Popper

Hook:	Stinger, sizes 3/0 to 10
Tail:	Marabou, hackle tips, Crystal Flash optional
Hackle:	Dyed or natural chicken hackle
Rubber Legs:	White or various colors, round or flat
Body:	Soft foam, flat end forward
Eyes:	Optional, doll eyes with stem
Weedguard:	Optional, stiff monofilament, diameter matches hook diameter

The beauty of the foam popper is that you get the pleasure of tying the popper with a minimum of fuss. There are two types of foam available, a soft foam that some feel is more "fishy" because when bass bite it, the foam gives a little, seducing bass with its more "lifelike" feel. The other foam is hard, but I suspect that a highly scientific study of number of seconds that bass spend munching on poppers would reveal that the crunchiness of a surface popper is less important than where the hook impales itself in the bony mouth of a bass. (Hard foam poppers are covered under Cork/Hard Foam Popper, page 12).

Tying Tips

The Stinger hook was originally developed as an extra long, extra wide gap hook to overcome the bulkiness of many poppers. Another theory held that poppers hook more bass with a wide gap, but I've found that isn't necessarily true, unless you hunt really big bass, and then you need to be careful because the wire in many Stinger hooks is too soft. I catch most of my bass with size 6 and 10 poppers. (There is a great deal of variance between manufacturers in defining hook sizes, however.)

As an option, for bass of less than three pounds, you can use almost any large gap, long shank streamer hook, particularly if the wire is strong.

I prefer using the pre-formed EdgeWater heads to tie foam poppers; however, you can make your own heads with foam blocks and a head shaping tool available from EdgeWater (1-800-584-7647). The EdgeWater foam heads are reversible: put the narrow end at the hook eye, you have a slider; put the fat end forward and you have a popper. They also market chugger and the boilermaker heads, that are more deeply dished. EdgeWater foam color variations include black, white, chartreuse, yellow, purple and blue.

Be sure to center the hole where hook eye goes through foam, using a needle with the same diameter as the hook wire, or the needle available from EdgeWater. To secure the foam use Zap-A-Gap cyanoacrylate super glue or EdgeWater's Aron Alpha super glue.

Variations

An important variation is the soft foam pencil popper, an elongated version of the standard popper, and one often used to simulate a wounded fish.

To get the hackle tips in the tail to flare outward, use a feather from each side of the neck; pluck a feather from the right and one from the left. When tied in back to back, their natural curvature will cause them to flare outward, giving the fly a scissoring motion in the water.

To reduce bulk when using smaller flies for bass, you can eliminate the flared hackle tips, or even the hackle wrapped behind the popper body. You can use Crystal Flash and just use a short tuft of marabou. One of the great advantages of a reduced fly is that you can use a light fly rod.

Fishing Tips

Soft foam poppers act differently in the water than cork, deer, or hard foam poppers; they are less dense and respond differently on the retrieve. Besides being easy to tie, they add another aspect to your fishing strategies.

I believe one of the true joys of fly fishing is tossing a popper at bass, both smallmouth and largemouth. Depending on their mood, bass take the topwater fly with gusto, blasting it in a surface explosion, boiling it as they suck it down, or inhaling your popper like a mason jar pulled underwater.

And there is no really bad way to present a popper. Sometimes I find bass want their meal in a certain way: real slow with quiet pops or a couple of medium pops and a pause, or maybe just a series of small pops. But most often, you can catch bass on poppers with whatever retrieve suits your fancy. And your fishing partner will probably catch bass doing it with a completely different retrieve. Whatever the case, you'll soon find that bass love to pop your popper.

1) Debarb hook, insert in vise. Attach thread, cover hook shank with thread. Start behind eye, working to the end of the shank, then back to the eye. Wrapping back towards the end of the shank again, go to where the foam head will end. This marks the spot where your materials will meet the end of the foam head. (The thread base helps the super glue bond to the foam.) (If adding optional weedguard, see page 4.) Tie in marabou tail (hook shank length) and trim excess. Add strands of optional Flashabou or Crystal Flash.

2) Tie in first tail feather so it curves outward, keeping it level with the hook or tipped slightly downward. (Feather extends hook shank length; stubs left on trimmed hackle allows thread to grip the stem better.) Tie in second tail feather to flair out on other side, matching its length and width to first tail feather. Trim excess and cement.

3) Tie in feather for hackle collar (width equals hook gap or a little more); stubs left on trimmed hackle allows thread to grip the stem better. (You may need two hackles.)

4) Wrap hackle around hook shank, tie off. Trim excess and cement.

5) Tie in rubber legs, (leaving room for weedguard tie-down behind hook eye). Whip finish and cement.

6) Using a thick needle, punch a centered hole through the foam. Check the fit by easing the foam onto the hook, over the eye, pointed-end-first, ending with the fat end just behind the hook eye. (You may need to cut some of the pointed end of the foam off to match the space left on the hook—be sure to leave enough space for the weedguard, if installed.) Apply Zap-A-Gap or Aron Alpha super glue to the thread-covered hook. Check foam to be sure it's centered over the hook. (Re-attach thread to finish optional weedguard, see page 4. Check foam body alignment.) For optional eyes: clip doll eye stem to one-fourth its length. Using a drill bit the same diameter as the doll eye stem, hand-twist the bit, forming a hole in the foam for the stem. Put a drop of super glue in the foam hole, insert doll eye stem into foam. Double check foam body for alignment. Trim rubber legs to hook shank length.

Soft Foam Slider

Hook:	Stinger, sizes 3/0 to 10
Tail:	Marabou; optional hackle tips, Crystal Flash
Hackle:	Dyed or natural chicken hackle as a collar
Rubber Legs:	White or various colors, round or flat
Body:	Soft foam, rounded end forward
Eyes:	Optional, doll eyes on stems
Weedguard:	Optional, stiff monofilament, diameter matches hook diameter

The slider is often overlooked in the fly fisher's arsenal. There are times when, even though they are in shallow water, bass are reluctant to smack a popper. If bass are just swirling or boiling under your popper but not taking it, switch to a slider. I've found that shallows bass that are hard fished, especially by popper flingers, will strike a slider. The slider slips underwater, swimming like bass prey, but without fish-alarming pops. Because they aren't scared of the slider, bass will strike it.

Tying Tips

I prefer using the pre-formed EdgeWater heads to tie soft foam sliders; however, you can make your own heads with foam blocks and a head shaping tool available from EdgeWater (1-800-584-7647). The EdgeWater foam heads are reversible: put the narrow end at the hook eye, you have a slider; put the fat end forward and you have a popper. EdgeWater foam color variations include black, white, chartreuse, yellow, purple and blue. (Hard foam sliders are covered under Cork/Hard Foam Slider, page 14).

Be sure to center the hole where hook eye goes through foam, using a needle with the same diameter as the hook wire, or the needle available from EdgeWater. To secure the foam use Zap-A-Gap cyanoacrylate super glue or EdgeWater's Aron Alpha super glue.

Variations

Doug Swisher and Bob Marvin of Naples, Florida, originally designed the Flute Fly, a slider variation that incorporates slots in the foam slider head. When you pull on the fly, some water scoots out of those slots, creating additional bass-attracting disturbance. EdgeWater also offers pre-formed Flute Fly heads.

I tie most of my sliders, and particularly the smaller ones, with just a marabou tail because I love its underwater mobility. If you desire more mass and movement in your slider, you can add a hackle collar and flared out hackle tips. The hackle is plucked from opposite sides of the neck; one feather from the right and one from the left side. When placed back to back, they flare out. (See Cork/Hard Foam Slider, page 18.) When you pull the slider towards you, the hackle tips flow together behind the fly, then when you pause the retrieve, the hackle tips flare out, a lifelike enticement for bass.

Fishing Tips

The foam popper is light and won't bury itself very far underwater, so you must fish it fairly slowly, allowing the marabou to undulate under the surface, teasing the bass to strike. Make several casts to each good looking spot, giving the bass plenty of time to decide to attack your slider. If the wind causes waves that make poppers less effective, use a slider. Retrieve your slider parallel to bass-hiding structure and also perpendicular to structure, so that no matter which way the bass is holding in its hiding place, it will see your slider easing along under the surface. Bass sometimes slide out to nail your slider, but they often smash it on a heavy strike.

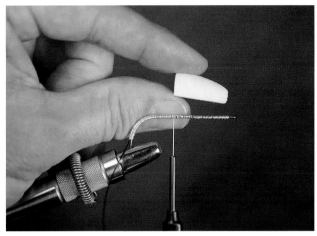

1) Debarb hook, insert in vise. Attach thread, cover hook shank with thread. Start behind eye, working to the end of the shank, then back to the eye. Wrapping back towards the end of the shank again, go to where the foam head will end. This marks the spot where your materials will meet the end of the foam head. (The thread base helps the super glue bond to the foam.) (If adding optional weedguard, see page 4.)

2) Tie on marabou (hook shank length) and optional Crystal Flash, trim excess and cement tie-down area.

3) Tie in optional collar hackle (width equals hook gap or a little more); stubs left on trimmed hackle allows thread to grip the stem better. (You may need two hackles.)

4) Wrap hackle around hook shank, tie off. Trim excess and cement.

5) Tie in rubber legs, (leaving room for weedguard tie-down behind hook eye). Whip finish and cement.

6) Using a thick needle, punch a centered hole through the foam. Check the fit by easing the foam onto the hook, over the eye, fat-end-first, ending with the pointed end just behind the hook eye. (You may need to cut some of the fat end of the foam off to match the space left on the hook—be sure to leave enough space for the weedguard, if installed.) Apply Zap-A-Gap or Aron Alpha super glue to the thread-covered hook. Check foam to be sure it's centered. (Re-attach thread to finish optional weedguard, see page 4.) For optional eyes: clip doll eye stem to one-fourth its length. Using a drill bit the same diameter as the doll eye stem, hand-twist the bit, forming a hole in the foam for the stem. Put a drop of super glue in the foam hole, insert doll eye stem into foam. Double check foam body for alignment. Trim rubber legs to hook shank length.

Wiggle Bug

Hook:	Wide gap, ring eye streamer hook, sizes 6-4/0 (Daiichi 2461 recommended)
Tail:	Marabou, varied colors; Crystal Flash, Flashabou optional
Hackle:	Optional body hackle
Body:	Foam, varied colors; chenille or yarn underbody
Eyes:	Optional, doll eyes with stem
Originated by:	Steve Shiba and Larry Tullis

There is no doubt that bass find wiggling, diving flies irresistible, and the Wiggle Bug does just that. Its underwater action is similar to a flatfish lure or any number of crankbaits. You can form your own Wiggle Bug body from beach sandal foam, but your best bet is to use the EdgeWater Wiggle Bug kit that includes the foam, hooks, and instructions, or buy the EdgeWater Wiggle Bug Sticks, which are the shaped foam bodies. (EdgeWater 1-800-584-7647) You may want to examine or purchase a completed fly, particularly for the placement of the foam on the hook.

Tying Tips

Be sure to center the hole where hook eye goes through foam, using a needle with the same diameter as the hook wire, or the needle available from EdgeWater. When tying in body material, be sure to leave plenty of room to insert the hook eye into the foam. To secure the foam use Zap-A-Gap cyanoacrylate super glue or EdgeWater's Aron Alpha super glue.

The Wiggle Bug is tied without a weedguard: the guard would hinder its swimming abilities; when fishing, if the Wiggle Bug hits a snag, the lip causes the fly to flip up over the obstacle, allowing you to continue the retrieve.

Variations

EdgeWater foam color variations include black, white, chartreuse, yellow, purple and blue. The underbody allows you some creative freedom because of the variety of materials and colors you can incorporate into the fly to entice bass. You can use yarn, chenille, sparkle chenille, dubbing, or pearlescent tubing over yarn or chenille. You can add body hackle or rib the fly with sparkle chenille or tinsel.

Fishing Tips

Use an open style knot that leaves a small loop of monofilament in front of the fly when you fish the Wiggle Bug, or it won't swim properly. Optionally, use a regular fly-to-tippet knot (such as an improved clinch knot) to tie on a small snap for attaching the Wiggle Bug.

If the Wiggle Bug doesn't swim straight, you can push the end of the diving lip to the side, modifying the swim path the bug will take when you retrieve the fly. Fishing the Wiggle Bug takes a bit more effort because the fly is bulky and its lip sticks out, slowing your cast. However, the Wiggle Bug isn't really all that much more work to cast than a large popper.

Retrieving the Wiggle Bug is demanding, because you must work the fly fairly fast to get it to dive and swim, particularly when fishing from a float tube or pontoon boat. You may need to pull your rod to the side while you strip line, and fin backwards if in a tube. The extra effort is well worth it, though, because bass attack the Wiggle Bug with gusto. Also, experiment with the retrieve, re-casting to a "bassy" area several times. I've had bass pounce on the Wiggle Bug as soon as it landed, but most bass need to see the fly swim to assault the Wiggle Bug as a meal.

1) Debarb hook, attach thread, wrap complete hook shank with thread, then apply cement. With thread at front of hook (leave room at the head for the foam), tie in body material (and optional hackle or ribbing). Trim excess, cement tie-down area.

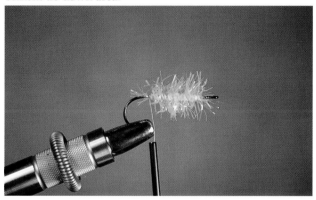

2) Wrap thread to the rear of the body. Wrap body to the rear, ending body just above the hook point (then the optional hackle or ribbing). Tie off, trim excess, cement tie-down area.

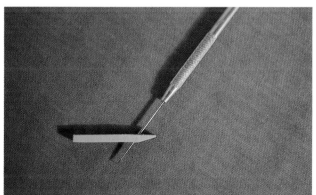

3) Hold the foam body so the flat side is up, then using a thick needle, puncture a hole in the foam. The needle must be: A) in the center of the foam; B) back from the front of the foam (the beveled part) the distance equal to the hook gap; C) angled to the rear at a 45 degree angle. (Foam will be turned over to install on the fly; you may need to shorten the foam to match the hook.)

4) Apply Zap-A-Gap or Aron Alpha super glue to the top of the body. With the lip to the front and pointing down and with beveled side down, slide the hole in the foam over the eye of the hook. Center the foam over the body and securely tie down, squashing foam. Thread is wrapped so some foam is to the rear of the tie-down spot; thread tie-down is centered over point of hook. While super glue is still flexible, make sure foam is centered over the hook.

5) Tie in marabou tail (about body length) on top of rear of foam, in same tie-down area as the previous step. (Tie in optional Flashabou or Crystal Flash.) Trim excess. Whip finish with Extended Reach Whip Finish tool. Cement tie-down area well. Remove fly from vise and check foam alignment.

6) Optional: install doll eyes (See Foam Slider, page 27, Step 6.)

About the Author

Deke Meyer is a full-time freelancer from Monmouth, Oregon, where he lives with his wife Barbara, who also fly fishes. He tied his first fly from a kit that arrived as a Christmas gift when he was 13 years old. His first size-10 fly had wings more suited for a size 6 fly. But with practice and working on the proper proportions, his flies got better and he caught fish. With the help of this book, and by remembering that fly tying is simply a matter of practice and proportion, you can tie flies that catch fish, too.

Deke's articles have been featured in most of the major fly fishing and outdoor magazines. His previous books include *Float Tube Fly Fishing*, *Advanced Fly Fishing For Steelhead*, *Saltwater Flies: Over 700 of the Best*, and the upcoming *McKenzie River Journal*. Previous books in this series include *Tying Trout Flies, 12 of the Best* and *Tying Trout Nymphs, 12 of the Best*, by Frank Amato Publications, Inc.

If you have any comments or would like to write to the author, he can be reached through the publisher at the following address:

Deke Meyer c/o Frank Amato Publications, Inc.
PO Box 82112
Portland, OR 97282

32